A NOVEL

Stefania Gander

MAYBE I'M NOT GOD
Cat Chronicles

Original Title: FORSE NON SONO DIO – Cronache di un gatto
First Italian Edition June 2024, First English Edition March
2025
Translated and Adapted from Italian by Chiara Gastaldi
email: chiara.cgastaldi@gmail.com
Graphic design, cover, editorial production and layout by
Gander Books ®
Copyright © Stefania Gander and Gander Books ®, 2024.
All rights reserved.
Published by Gander Books, Via Righi 9, 39100 Bolzano - Italy
Info@ganderbooks.it
www.ganderbooks.it
Phone +39 327 011 4115
ISBN 9791281230293

To Sabrina,
who has put up with and supported me
for over twenty years:
without her, neither this publishing house,
nor this book, nor this title
would ever have come to light.

To Cindy,
who left me far too soon
yet taught me
how much love a cat can give.
The final pages of this book
are inspired by her.

To Minou,
a source of inspiration for this book,
who ended her earthly journey
a few days before the release of this
English edition.

Introduction

I must admit I feel a bit uncomfortable signing this book.

Not so much because I am both its author and its publisher—writing occasionally is a little indulgence that more than one publisher allows themselves, and, in some ways, it's important to occasionally face the judgment of readers. Rather, my discomfort stems from the fact that it will be obvious to the sharpest of readers that this book is not entirely my doing.

Allow me to explain.

I am currently the proud mother of four cats, a statement that divides the world into two groups. On one side, those who do not have cats and, with a certain level of irritation, insist that cats are not children, that a clear distinction must be maintained between humans and felines, and that if people are having fewer children these days, it's partly because of people like me, who have found a surrogate for parenthood in our pets. On the other side, cat owners will simply smile and think, "I have two," or "I just have one," or "I, too, am a mom (or dad) to one, two, or more cats." The divide is sharp, almost ideological. But I digress.

For those belonging to the latter, it will quickly become apparent that I am, in truth, merely a translator of feline thought. It's as if, at night, in my dreams—or in that liminal space between sleep and wakefulness where we insomniacs nurture our projects, ideas, and confront a parallel reality unknown to sound sleepers—thousands of cats had transmitted their thoughts to me, entrusting me with the task of translating them into a language comprehensible to humans.

If you recognize parts of your own cats in the protagonist, then I will have succeeded in fulfilling this duty.

Since the feline protagonist of this book—whose name you will discover only by diving into its pages—represents all of our cats, it is he (though it could very well be she—"cat" here is used as a generic term) who has been entrusted with the task of revealing some of the secrets of the feline mind. It is he who takes us into their daily lives, explaining how our cats experience it. And, most importantly, it is he who recounts our world from a completely different perspective—one that does not conform to our logic, but to another. A perspective where the mental acrobatics of us humans are seen as almost incomprehensible oddities rather than the fruits of Darwinian evolution.

If, on the other hand, you do not own a cat and belong to the first category I mentioned earlier, you must read this book to understand how the other half of the world thinks—a half you will undoubtedly want to join by the end of this book.

Above all, however, this book is my great act of love for all those wonderful felines who have accompanied me and continue to accompany me in my daily life. They are indelibly etched in my memory, so that one day, when the time comes, I may meet them again and pet them for all eternity.

Catnapping

You scoundrels, leave me alone! I said let me go... stop grabbing my scruff, or I'll bite you, I'll destroy you, I'll annihila... Moooommm... Don't you dare, I'm not kidding—if you don't stop, I'll become a fury, I'll scratch you until there's nothing lef... Nooo, don't do it! I don't want this, let me go... I was joking, okay? I won't do anything. Look, I'm staying still—see how still I am? Perfectly still. The stillest cat you have ever seen. I'm being so good. So, why don't you just put me back with my mom, and we can all pretend this never happened, huh?

No one needs to know, and we'll all be friends again. Deal?

Mom... where are you? Please come here, come get me! They've put me in a cage and they're taking me away. Mom...

They've kidnapped me. Maybe they're cat-nappers.

I miss you, Mom.

The Gang

I spent my first night away from Mom.

The catnappers are professionals; clearly, this operation isn't their first time. They brought me to their hideout and set me free—well… "free"; let's say they opened the door of the cage they'd been keeping me in—and left me in a room, alone.

Every five minutes, one of the gang members comes to check on me. I've tried everything to escape, but they're clever. They're also annoyingly unshakable. I hissed, arched my back, and gave them my most menacing glare, but it didn't work. They're too strong. They just pick me up like it's nothing, and every so often, they carry me up to their mouths where, making strange noises, they press weird things against my head and nose. They call them "kisses." I think it's some kind of psychological torture they've devised to instill fear.

But what scares me the most is that they've said—more than once—that they could just eat me.

I fear for my life. At first, I thought these people had catnapped me to demand a ransom, but now I'm seriously afraid I might be food. My life is in real danger.

I also need to figure out who "Kitty" is. They keep calling that name regularly. I suspect it's some kind of guard assigned to make sure I don't escape, but despite my careful searches, I haven't seen anyone by that name.

I'll try harder to investigate in the next few hours, but right now I'm exhausted. I've only managed to sleep thirteen hours today, and the fatigue is catching up with me.

I miss Mom, but I'm so focused on planning my escape that I can't even think about her right now.

The Doubt

The catnappers are treating me well: the food is good—a little too good, I'd say. Unfortunately, they keep touching me, picking me up, and covering me with that awful thing they do with their mouths. I suspect they might be fattening me up to eat me later. Maybe I should cut back on the food to delay the inevitable, but if I'm wrong, it would be a shame to waste all those delicacies. So, just to be safe, I keep eating.

For a few hours, they gave me a wonderful cardboard box to sleep in, but they took it away and replaced it with some kind of fabric contraption. It's all colorful and covered in useless little patterns. Clearly, in this place, my cherished sense of simplicity is not shared.

I think I've also heard, beyond the door keeping me locked in this room, meows and other feline sounds. If that's the case, I have to conclude that this is a highly organized gang specializing in cat abductions. I find myself hoping it's not a criminal ring trafficking wholesale cat meat—if so, my fate is sealed.

Still no sign of "Kitty," who might actually be "Kitty-kitty," or even "Here-kitty-kitty." I'm fairly convinced they must be somewhere in this room. I'll keep looking, but after I sleep.

Sweet dreams to you too, Mom, wherever you are. Although… I'm starting to forget what you looked like. Maybe I'm still too young to remember things clearly. And besides, I'm so sleepy.

Escape

I've escaped. They opened the door, and I was hiding close by, so the moment there was enough space, I bolted.

I noticed the catnappers have trouble reaching covered spots and tight corners, so I took full advantage of that. During my getaway, I ran into another cat who looks a lot like... what's her name... oh yeah, that kind one that used to give me milk... "Mom," I think. But she hissed at me, arched her back, puffed up her tail. If you ask me, she hasn't been catnapped— she might be a collaborator.

Anyway, this place is huge; you can really run around and find good hiding spots.

I can hear them looking for me, calling out "Kitty-kitty" (which might actually be the nickname of "HereKittyKitty"). I still haven't seen him, but I'm sure he's some shady character who lurks in the shadows. I admit the thought of meeting him makes me a little nervous.

For now, I'm hidden in a little corner under what might be a chest—though I'm not too familiar with this kind of thing, so I can't say for sure. I need to think about my next moves, figure out how I can return... speaking of which, return where? I don't really remember where I came fr...—Oh no, there they are! They've spotted me, and the female two-legged one is crouching down to grab me... You won't catch me that easily, so I'll hiss, I'll scratch, I'll bite... hey, let go of my scruff! Why do you always grab me there? Fine, I'll behave, I'll stay very, very still... actually, this feels like déjà-vu.

They've got me. They're probably going to eat me now. I'm almost certain I'm about to die.

Stop

Yesterday's escape did the trick: apparently, my bold, brazen attitude spooked the bandits because this morning they opened the door voluntarily, leaving me free to explore.

I got to see just how big this place is, and how many interesting things there are—naturally, I had to test them all out. I have to say, the catnappers didn't share my enthusiasm for trial and error. When I climbed the cloth flaps hanging in front of the windows or tested the durability of some plastic material covering the table (which dangled off the edge), they forced me to stop. The same thing happened when I tried to stretch my paws and sink my claws into a sort of seat which looked super comfortable and which I plan to test again soon.

However, I was able to guess what my name is: "Stop." Short, to the point, and easy to memorize. I actually like it. Although it could be the short form of *Stopmonkeyingaroundgetdownfromthere* which they've used on me a few times. I'll try to figure that out in the coming days.

As for the collaborators, there are two of them. One is a young adult cat, kind of stuck-up and irritating—also easily irritated—while the other is that older-looking cat I ran into during my escape. She limps noticeably and keeps hissing at me, although I think it's more out of habit or maybe because it's part of her job description. Deep down, she seems really sweet, and I like her a lot. She reminds me of someone, though I can't say exactly who, but whenever I see her, I feel good inside. I'll try getting closer to her at the next opportunity. Something tells me she won't push me away.

The food here is still good, and I have to admit, these catnappers don't seem so bad. Maybe they catnapped me because they needed a ransom—maybe they're broke—and that rules out the possibility of them wanting to eat me. In fact, it's probably safe to say they don't eat cats at all, which is kind of a relief.

I even have my very own box filled with sand, and the astonishing part is that the cat-nappers clean it for me! I find that quite extraordinary, and I suspect it's thanks to the intimidating stance I took yesterday.

Still no sign of "HereKittyKitty" or just "Kitty," and that's starting to seriously bother me. Why don't I ever see them?

Kitty

I'll destroy you. I'll wreck your house, bite your jugular in your sleep, sink my claws right in the middle of your eye!

How dare you? I have my dignity, my pride. I descend from Egyptian cat dynasties, worshipped like gods! My relatives are forest kings, striking terror everywhere on the planet, and you dare tell me my name is "Kitty"?

Do you realize how offensive that is? And not just that! You even say "Kitty-kitty" or "HereKittyKitty." For the record, I'd take "Stop" over that any day. I could have lived with something like "Ramses," "Simba," or

"Shere Khan," but "Kitty" is an insult I absolutely do not deserve.

I'm exhausted. I'm going to sleep. But when I wake up, I'm throwing up on the rug.

The Boss

The old cat keeps hissing at me whenever she sees me, but she seems a lot less committed to it than before. Maybe she's getting used to me. Yesterday I tried biting her back legs in jest while she was walking, but she didn't appreciate it one bit. I won't do it again, but I still want to get closer to her—she inspires trust.

The younger cat seems way more annoyed, though. He's been hiding under the bed all day, and the two-legs keep trying to coax him out, making weird mouth noises. They even change their voices when they call him (I think his name is "ComeonFelixgetoutofthere"), and frankly, it all seems a bit stupid to me. The mere fact that they have to speak to communicate strikes me as not particularly intelligent, but speaking in those silly tones is next-level weird.

Anyway, I'm starting to doubt my original theory about them wanting to eat me or demand a ransom. I mean, I can't even remember where exactly I was taken from, and aside from all their shouting (which happens way more often than I'd like), they're actually pretty attentive. They communicate with noises, so I've discovered that all I have to do is meow, and they'll bring me kibble—kibble they must hunt for every morning when they leave and come back hours later.

I'm not entirely sure how you catch kibble or where it's found, but they're good at it, because they never run out. And it tastes pretty great.

Then, if I meow differently, they stop whatever they're doing and scratch my back or give me tummy rubs, which are lovely.

Sometimes I think I'm actually the one in charge around here.

God

Today was terrible—I was absolutely terrified. I was dozing on that thing they call a couch when suddenly the male two-leg grabbed me, stuck me in the same cage they used when I got here (I'm not sure anymore if it was a catnapping or just them bringing me home), then slammed some sort of hatch and lifted me off the ground to take me outside. It's noisy out there; big things rush by at crazy speeds, and the air smells awful.

They shoved me into one of those fast-moving things—seems like the same one I arrived in—and off we went.

I yelled at the top of my lungs, but they wouldn't turn around or open the cage. So partly out of fear and partly out of spite, I did my business right there in the cage.

The two-legs started complaining, then opened some windows to let in high-speed air, and the male two-leg got mad at some "Todd," or "Rod" or "whatever," blaming him for the smell. Maybe they didn't realize I was the culprit. Then again, I haven't seen this "Todd" at all, and given previous experiences (like that "KittyKitty" nonsense), I hope they're not actually talking about me. Another ridiculous name is the last thing I need.

Anyway, we arrived at this horrible place that smells acrid and unbearable. I tried to escape, but a bearded man in glasses and a long white coat grabbed me firmly, started prying my eyelids open, checking my ears, placing some thing on my chest, and then—he pulled out what had to be a weapon and stabbed me. I felt it go into my body, injecting something.

I thought I was a goner. Maybe I was wrong all along, and they really do want to eat me. Maybe this was the end. But somehow—maybe because I'm strong and I descend from a king of the forest—I survived.

But I was terrified. They put me back in the cage, which at that point felt safer than being out in the open, and I curled up inside it. Then we took that fast thing home again.

Once again, I did my business in the cage, and once again the male two-leg yelled at that "Todd," or maybe "God"—I'm not sure—and it made the female two-leg angry, which suggests she might have figured out it was me and not this "God".

But since I didn't see this "God" in the car, and remembering the fiasco with "KittyKitty," I can't help wondering if they're once again talking about me.

Now I'm completely worn out, but tomorrow I need to make sure it's not another "Kitty" situation, where I wake up and discover that maybe I am God!

The Flight

It wasn't supposed to end like this. It was supposed to be a game—we'd have fun, a few laughs. The male two-leg's feet were sticking out from under the blanket; you couldn't miss them.

The biggest toe stood out among the others, serving no apparent purpose other than being my target. So, I crept toward it, careful not to make a sound or disturb the nighttime silence—didn't want him to move that toe out of sight and ruin my chance to win the match. Or at least, what I assumed was a match, though now I'm not so sure.

It was motionless, a prey so easy it almost felt too convenient. When I was a few inches away, I pounced, landing on the big toe. It was a fraction of a second. I pinned it down with my claws and gave it a little nibble to seal my victory.

What happened next is a blur. I'd noticed two-legs don't handle losing very well, but I wasn't prepared for this.

A sudden jolt, powerful and decisive. And a shout. The room started spinning, I felt myself graze the wardrobe about two meters from the bed, desperately trying to find some kind of midair balance. I finally stopped spinning. I hope I land properly!

A New Mama

I did it. Finally.

Mimi, that's definitely the old cat's name (clearly, creativity in naming cats isn't high on these humans' priority list) was curled up on the couch, right in the corner. She was in a deep sleep, and I could tell because Mimi snores loudly when she's out cold. So, I jumped lightly onto the couch and inched closer, careful not to wake her. When she's awake, she still hisses at me—though less than before.

Once I got really close, I curled up and pressed my whole body against hers. Mimi woke up and looked at me, startled. I expected her to hiss, and maybe she was tempted to do so at first, but she just stared at me for a few seconds and then started grooming me: licking my head, really getting behind my ears, even putting a paw on my head so I couldn't move while she washed my face. (Not that I wanted to move—I felt so good, I wouldn't have fled even if I could.)

It's been a long time since I felt this kind of warmth. I vaguely remember feeling it before, but I can't picture exactly when. Mimi kept grooming me, caring for me, while I relaxed into loud purrs. As I basked in bliss, a word popped into my head—"Mama". I think I should remember something about that word, but I can't quite bring it into focus. I only know that whenever I look at Mimi, that word comes to me without me even trying.

I'm not totally sure, but I think Mimi might be my mama, and I really, really love that idea. Actually, I adore it.

Adoption?

When both two-legs noticed that Mimi was grooming me and that she'd stopped hissing at me, started making weird noises that sounded like delight. They approached us and started petting me and Mama on our heads.

It felt incredible. I purred the entire time—and loudly, at that.

In fact, these two-legs don't seem evil. Nor do they look like they're planning a ransom (I'm certain at this point they don't plan to eat me). So now I'm wondering: what if I wasn't catnapped? What if I was adopted?

I need to find out. I really hope that's the case.

The Bed

I slept on the two-legs' bed. I'd been meaning to go for it for a while—that bed seems to be the softest spot in the whole house—but it was complicated by the fact that Felix and Mama already sleep there. If I knew Mama wouldn't mind, I wasn't so sure about Felix. I'd have to be determined to get my share of bed space.

I waited until the dead of night, once everyone was asleep. Then, trying not to make noise, I jumped onto a corner of the bed. I could have chosen a free corner near their feet, but I considered that too risky: Felix might spot me before I could settle in. So, I climbed up where the male two-leg rests his head. Carefully, stepping over the male's face, then the female's face, I found a perfect vantage point and spotted an ideal, actually perfect, nook where I could curl up—exactly between the two two-legs' pillows.

That way, not only did Felix not notice me, but both two-legs—woken up by me strolling across their faces—began to cuddle me and even give me little kisses (which I have to admit I enjoy more than I did a few weeks ago).

They're kind of weird, though: if someone walked on my face, I'd claw them silly. Instead, they seem delighted. At any rate, I slept wonderfully, and when I woke up, Felix was no longer on the bed. I hope he's not mad or planning to pull any stunts, because there are still tensions between us that we'll eventually need to address—one way or another.

Maybe I'm Not God

Today has been another extremely tough day. The male two-leg tricked me, grabbed me with brute force, and shoved me into the portable prison. I tried to fight back—even used my claws—but all I managed was to leave a tiny scratch on his hand and earn a big shout where he once again invoked "God."

Then, as before, he put me in that fast-moving box I despise. And, as before, I protested by relieving myself in the absence of a decent litter box, and once again he yelled out for this "God," who is apparently both "his" and "dear," sounding exasperated. At this point, though, I'm starting to think that maybe I'm not God; instead he's my accomplice, since he always takes the blame for my mistakes, or at least the two-leg seems to think so, otherwise, this bitterness wouldn't make sense.

Anyway, they dragged me back to that smelly place, and the bearded guy in glasses gave me a shot. I passed out.

I woke up not long after, back in the mobile box, feeling totally groggy. Now I'm home. I'm still out of it, and there's something weird going on under my tail—like something's missing. The two two-legs keep showering me with affection, which makes it a bit easier to bear, although they should have fed me by now and I don't see any kibble around. I suspect they weren't able to hunt for kibble because they were with me. Then again, I'm not super hungry. I'm just really sleepy, so I think I'll drift off now, wrapped in all these cuddles.

The Tree

I think two-legs need to learn how to handle frustration with more grace, and more importantly, if they can't handle losing, they shouldn't play.

Today, the two-legs arrived with a tree. A weird move, but it piqued my curiosity. They set it up in the living room, and to my surprise, they started hanging colorful balls on it.

At first, I just watched. Then I tried to get closer, but they pushed me away. I tried again, but they blocked me. So, I tried once more, quicker this time, and they chased me off so I couldn't get near it. That's when it all clicked:

they were placing balls on the tree, and I was supposed to knock them off! (I mean, what's the point of sticking balls on a fir tree-especially lighting them up so they're even more visible-if not to lure me into swatting them down?) And it was their job to keep me from doing exactly that. I even wondered if each color had a different point value, but I can't count, so I didn't stress about it.

For most of the evening, they had the upper hand. I noticed a competitive streak in them that I've rarely seen before. They really moved skillfully, guarding the tree and the ornaments. But I knew sooner or later they'd have to throw in the towel—and that's exactly what happened. Eventually, they turned off all the lights, apparently convinced that I wouldn't be able to spot the target in the dark and went off to bed.

A rookie mistake I couldn't pass up. On silent paws, I crept up to the tree, climbed to the top, then worked my way down, knocking the balls off one by one. (Kind of a bummer they shattered when they hit the floor; if they'd bounced, we could have had a lot more fun with them.) Alarmed by the unmistakable sounds of my victory, both two-legs sprang out of bed in a futile last-ditch attempt to prevent defeat.

My victory was absolute, with most of the balls lying on the floor. Yet instead of congratulating me on such a feat—which, if you ask me, clearly deserved a treat or two (that special kibble they call "treats")—they started scolding me and my mysterious yet ever-reliable accomplice, chasing me in a threatening manner.

While dashing off to hide under a piece of furniture, I caught the disapproving glare of Mama and Felix. Apparently, they know how the two-legs react to losing, so they hadn't joined in the game.

I'll admit it stung a bit. It's a side of the two-legs I hadn't seen and wasn't expecting.

If that's how they handle defeat, so be it. I won't play anymore. They can keep their tree—I'm not going near it again!

Maybe.

Overly Emotional

She's eating too much. And she's gaining weight. I don't know what's up with the female two-leg—sure, hunting kibble every day might be stressful (although they don't even eat the kibble themselves, go figure), but maybe she should get a grip on her emotions. I'm no expert, but overeating rarely solves your problems. Especially since, besides eating and putting on pounds, sometimes she cries for no reason, randomly laughs, and often fails to keep down what she's eaten.

The male two-leg, meanwhile, is ridiculously attentive to her every need, indulging her in ways that, if you ask me, are creating a kind of codependency that won't lead to anything good. There are five of us in this house; we all deserve some peace and privacy. This is messing with our harmony. I really hope this whole drama doesn't last for months because it's getting tiresome.

The Balcony

Days are getting longer. In the evening, it is still light outside, and for a few hours, the two-legs open the balcony door for us. While we still have unresolved issues we'll need to face at some point, Felix and I go out on the balcony—Mama rarely goes out anymore.

Felix and I bask in the sun. I personally love sitting right on the railing, even though the two-legs—no idea why—turn pale when they see me perched there and forcibly yank me down. It's really annoying, because it spoils all the fun, as I do so love peering down from up high. So, out of spite, I go inside and snuggle up to Mama, who's always sweet, licking me and showering me with affection, even though she moves less and less these days and struggles to get around.

Still, she's so soft, and when I curl up next to her, I feel safe and content like nowhere else. I wish she'd come outside to enjoy the warm sun, too, but by now she's set in her ways and spends most of her time sleeping. Yes, so do I, but she sleeps even more—much more than I do.

Outside

I don't want to cause a scene, so I won't say much- I won't be vulgar; mistakes happen, and I don't want to come off as some prissy perfectionist—but... If you ever lock me out on the balcony again when you leave to hunt kibble, leaving me without water, food, or a litter box for four hours, I will become your worst nightmare! You can check before you leave, can't you? Isn't it worth a few seconds of your time to make sure you're not abandoning one of us to starve to death?

And don't assume you can fix things by simply cleaning up what I was forced to do out there or by giving me treats and cuddles afterward... oh, by the way, scratch me just behind the left ear... yeah, that's it, good work, keep going...

Also, dear Felix,—I realize our relationship still has some murky corners we're pretending will resolve themselves, but walking right past the balcony door as the two-legs close it—fully aware I'm still outside—and acting like nothing's happening? That's low. You could've at least meowed and let them know I was out there, instead of leaving me to holler my head off for the entire neighborhood to hear.

And now that I think about it, those chuckles from the two-legs while they pick me up and smother me with kisses to soothe their own guilt? Not very classy. Show some respect, please. More respect!

Visions

There's something there. I can't say exactly what, but something's there. When I stand on that specific tile and stare at a certain distant spot, I see something.

It's blurry and chaotic—like shadows, lots of shadows, dancing around. The two-legs don't understand; I can tell from how they look at me and laugh when I concentrate, trying to decipher these visions that feel so real, yet so hazy. They can't see them, but I know Felix and Mama sense them, too. And although I still haven't truly figured out what I'm seeing, I have the feeling it's something wonderful. In fact, I'm certain of it.

Water

What you're doing to me is unacceptable, unfair, ridiculous, and downright cruel.

My only crime is liking running water. You know that about me and, to your credit, every morning you turn the faucet on so I can drink. Last night you didn't come home, deciding to leave me to die of thirst right there in front of the faucet, waiting for someone to show up and turn on the water.

Well, guess what? I've seen how you raise that lever to get the water flowing, and I've learned to do it myself. And I drank.

And let's not start blaming the sink stopper, okay? All I did was place a paw on a stopper that is logically supposed to stop water from draining. Then again, we're back to your weirdness: why put a stopper in a drain if you don't actually want to block it? Don't put it there in the first place! Or if you must, don't expect me to understand your illogical ways. If you didn't have the stopper, which would've made sense to me, the house wouldn't have flooded, and I wouldn't be stuck with an angry Mom scolding me for being "naughty."

I don't deserve this. So, I'm going to vomit somewhere, but I haven't decided where just yet. But rest assured, I will.

Fear

I'm scared. Really scared. My paw hurts, and I don't like all these noises. I want to go back to Mama on the couch.

I'm not sure how it happened. I was on the railing, enjoying the sun, and suddenly—just like that—I fell. I managed to twist midair and land on all four feet, but I landed hard on my right back leg, and now I'm hiding under a big shrub.

Cars are zooming by, making a terrible noise that reminds me of when they take me to get shots from the guy in the white coat, only much, much louder.

I saw my two two-legs walking around, calling me (and, seriously, can we not yell "Kitty-kitty" in the street like that?), but I'm too scared to come out. What if something happens to me on the way back to them? How can I trust anything with all this racket? Where do I find the courage to go to Mom and Dad?

Oh my gosh, I just called the two-legs Mom and Dad! And what about my cat mama? I'm mixing everything up, but right now I need a two-leg mom and dad, too. I need them to save me and bring me home.

Return

The noise has died down, but now it's late at night and I'm still terrified. I can see Mom and Dad two-legs in the distance, shining lights around, but they haven't found me. I don't know what to do—I'm shaking with fear.

Maybe I should meow? Usually, they come when I meow... maybe they haven't heard me yet. Let me try a little louder... That seems to be working—I think they're coming closer... Louder, louder... Yes, there they are!

Dad, what are you doing? You're picking me up, just like that? I need to figure out what's out here! Wait, I'm not ready, I'm still scared... and again with the scruff… Why do they always grab me there? But at least I'm in his arms now. Dad, please take me home so I can see Mama Cat.

It's almost morning by the time we get back. Finally, I'm home. I'm curled up against Mama Cat while she licks me clean. I've already eaten a dish of kibble, and Mom and Dad two-legs are petting me and kissing me all over.

The night is ending, and my fear is fading. Soon the sun will rise again, and I'll be back out on the balcony, soaking up the sun, on the railing, where else?

Vacation

Well, well, look who decided to come back. Congratulations. And now you expect me to greet you after you two crooks—yes, crooks, let's use the right words—disappeared for two whole weeks?

What's shocking is that the day before you vanished, you set out these amazing boxes, filled them with soft clothes, and took them with you. Naturally, I lay down in one of those lovely boxes, but instead of being happy and seizing the chance to bring me along, you threw me out of the box and wouldn't let me back in.

So, the two-legs deliberately chose to deprive themselves of my presence for fourteen days!

Luckily, the two older female two-legs, who often come around, took turns bringing kibble, refilling the water bowl, and cleaning our litter boxes. But really—forcing two elderly ladies to go off hunting for kibble? I still haven't figured out where it grows in the wild, but judging by how long it takes them to gather it, it can't be an easy task.

Now you Mom and Dad want to cuddle me—meanwhile, the female two-leg looks like she's about to burst (what on earth has she been eating?)… Really, do you think I'm going to let you bribe me with some petting? This time you've gone too far. Go on with your "HereKittyKitty," I'm staying under this bed until tomorrow.

Worries

I'm worried. Partly because I saw a box full of clothes similar to the one they used when they disappeared for two weeks, only smaller, and partly because I saw them rush out this morning with the female two-leg clearly unwell. I've been thinking for a while that she's gotten way too big, but I haven't figured out how to let her know.

I also noticed Mama Mimi and Felix were worried, too, so the three of us curled up together for a nap.

Oh, wait—I hear someone on the stairs... but it sounds like just one two-leg. It's Dad, and the female two-leg isn't with him. I knew she was sick... Although Dad looks happy, which is odd. Then again, I gave up trying to fully understand two-legs a long time ago. They're just too strange.

News

What kind of magic is this? And what is that thing over there?

The female two-leg is back, but she doesn't even look like herself—she's lost a ton of weight. I don't know how she did it, but it's hard to imagine dropping that many pounds by just fasting a couple of days.

And what did they bring in that basket? They haven't shown me or Felix or Mama Mimi. I just hear occasional wails and smell something weird—could be milk, if only I could remember exactly what milk smells like.

Oh, here goes the female two-leg showing us…

What is that? Why is it all wrapped in pink? It's way too small to be a two-leg—it can't even stand up. Is it a cat? Another cat, as if the three of us weren't enough? Its face is kind of funny, just a touch less pink than that stuff it's wrapped in. Clearly, the two-legs are over the moon about it, which means they're paying a little less attention to us. I hope it's just the novelty effect, because I don't like being sidelined—even though, to be fair, I don't mind a little peace and quiet to do my own thing.

Still, let's not go overboard…

The Monster

This is not going well.

Sure, I can deal with that pink thing—which I'm absolutely certain is called "Grandma's-little-sweetheart-come-here," because both of the older female two-legs refer to it that way. Fine, it might look like some big deal to them, though I'm starting to doubt it's very bright and I'm not convinced it's a cat. By now it should at least be able to move around on its own. Fine, I'll accept that here we often get only quick, halfhearted cuddles, sometimes grudgingly. But this time, they've really crossed the line.

They locked me, Mama Mimi, and Felix in a room so we can't leave. Some friends of the two-legs arrived to see "Grandma's-little-sweetheart-come-here," but they brought along a four-legged monster. It's definitely not a cat—it reeks so badly we can smell it through the door—and it has serious breath issues. All it does is wag its tail and follow basic commands from the visiting two-legs. When it saw us, it made these harsh, angry, low-pitched and non-sensical noises, presumably to scare us.

Mama Mimi and Felix fled immediately. As for me, they grabbed me just in time, since I was already hissing, back arched, tail puffed out, ready to leap at that beast and show who's really in charge around here.

In any case, the result is that we're now locked in a room in our own home, while that monster - I've seen similar creatures before at the place with the man in the white coat who tried to stab me with a needle - roams free.

I need to show Mom and Dad two-leg that I don't require this kind of "protection." I can take care of myself. And if they're not up to the job of kicking that monster out, well, I certainly am.

A Pointless Tree

A few days ago, another tree popped up in the house.

A fake one.

So basically, a tree-shaped object that looks like a tree but isn't actually a tree. It doesn't even have a real wooden trunk to scratch. Nothing.

To make matters worse, there are no colorful balls like last time. Instead, they hung some colored lights that don't even work properly— they keep blinking on and off, on and off. I have no idea what kind of "game" this is supposed to be—nothing about it seems fun to me, but if they're happy, fine. They've also placed a bunch of closed boxes on the floor, wrapped in bright paper with pretty bows that I'm not allowed to touch—so what are they for? Again, what's the point? They had a few boxes before, but now there's a whole mountain. As usual, these two-legs have no sense of moderation or balance. Frankly, I just don't get it at all.

Mimi

I don't think Mama Mimi is doing well. I curled up next to her because, even though I'm grown now, I still love napping with my head resting on her side, and I can tell she's having trouble breathing.

She has lost a lot of weight, limps more and more, and barely eats or drinks. She throws up more often, too. Sometimes she meows like she's in pain, and she struggles even to lick me a bit on the head and ears, which I love. I tried grooming her instead, hoping she enjoyed it at least a little. Mom and Dad two-leg are cuddling her a lot, and for the first time in months, they're spending more time with her than with "Grandma's-little-sweetheart-come-here."

Two-legs don't meow. They make sounds—some I understand, some I don't—and use those sounds to communicate with us and with each other. But when they're really unwell or sad, they make quieter sounds while salty water drips from their eyes and flows down their faces. I think they call it a "dontcry". Whenever it happens to someone, the others immediately point it out by saying *dontcry*—even though, honestly, I think two-legs must already know when they're having a *dontcry*. Even Grandma's-little-sweetheart-come-here does it sometimes, though she's much louder, while the grown two-legs are more subdued.

Today is the first time I've seen both of them having a *dontcry* at the same time, and neither of them is pointing it out to the other. They're just sitting there, petting Mama Mimi, absorbed in their *dontcry*.

Dontcry

They left this morning—all three of them: Dad, the mom two-leg, and Mama Mimi.

Mama Mimi was in terrible shape. I spent the whole night by her side, and at some point Felix showed up, too—he's usually so reserved he hardly ever sleeps with us. Early in the morning, Dad said something into the little box he's always talking to and constantly holding in his hand, then he talked to the female two-leg, who was immediately overwhelmed by a *dontcry* and Dad pointed it out, telling her *dontcry*—but then he started having a *dontcry* himself, and soon they were both standing there, hugging each other, lost in their *dontcry*.

I tried grooming Mama Mimi on the head and ears—she usually likes that—but she just stared at me with this tired, exhausted look, as if she hadn't slept for months. Then the female two-leg came and picked her up. The moment I lost physical contact with her, I had the dreadful feeling it was forever—that I'd never have it again.

The female two-leg held Mama Mimi tightly against her chest, then Dad came and hugged them both. Soon after, the older female two-leg (the one Dad calls "Mom") arrived and had a *dontcry* too—though a bit less than them.

Before leaving with Mama Mimi in her arms, Mom and Dad two-legs brought her over to me and Felix. I rubbed my face against her, and so did Felix. Mama Mimi looked at us, and we could tell she liked it, even though she looked unusually tired.

Then they left, and Felix and I stayed there on the couch. Neither of us felt like moving. After a long while, Mom and Dad two-leg came back, but Mama Mimi wasn't with them.

They came over to me and Felix, Mom scooped me up, Dad scooped Felix up, and they showered us with kisses like never before. Then they brought "Grandma's-little-sweetheart-come-here" over to the couch with us, and the older female two-leg joined in. They all stayed there, petting and cuddling us, absorbed in their *dontcry* the whole time.

They were really sad, and so was I. I wanted Mama Mimi here. I wanted to curl up beside her and have her clean my head and ears. I thought maybe she'd come back without me and Felix noticing, so I got off the couch to look around.

I thought maybe she'd slipped back into the house unseen, so I hopped off the couch and searched every corner. But she wasn't there. She hadn't come home with Mom and Dad. I returned to the couch and just stared at nothing. Mama Mimi was gone, and I knew she'd never be back.

Sphynx

I'm a bit confused. Today, Alice—that's the nickname they use for "Grandma's-little-sweet-heart-come-here," which was definitely too long—was crawling around on all fours. This is the first time she's moved on her own, and I'm not sure if I'm more stunned by how long it took for her to gain her mobility or simply by seeing her move at all.

I still haven't figured out exactly what she is. She's not a two-leg, because she's tiny and doesn't move like them, but she's not a cat, either...

Yet here she is... hairless... pink... needing to be covered up so she doesn't freeze... she's on all fours... I'm not entirely sure, but with reasonable confidence, I'd say Alice is a Sphynx!

Hideout

Felix went into hiding. Well, not exactly—he thinks he's hiding. Alice won't stay still for a second, and the moment they set her on the floor, she starts moving around. Only Mom managed to stop her from playing in my litter box, which I would've found rather annoying: there's a reason I cover up my business!

After failing to get into my litter box, Alice spotted Felix and decided to go after him. Felix froze until she smacked him on the back, making him run away. But since Alice kept chasing him, he decided to hide. In a corner. With his face turned to the wall. Visible as a lighthouse in the night—basically the perfect target. And, sure enough, Alice had no trouble finding him.

At the Table!

I've never understood why I have to eat on the floor while the two-legs eat at a table—especially since I'm the one who loves heights. Unfortunately, every time I try to jump up to what I consider my rightful spot (the center of the table), they shoo me down in a manner I can only describe as authoritarian and despotic.

Now, though, Alice—who showed up *after* I did—also eats at the table, but she isn't held to the same rules that Felix and I are. Felix, of course, doesn't seem too bothered by this, but then again, you can't expect a brilliant response from someone who thinks hiding means facing a wall. The point is, while Alice sits at the table during meals, I'm forbidden from climbing onto it even when there's no food around. I've never tolerated that.

But the point is, while Alice can be at the table with the two-legs during meals, I'm forbidden from even jumping on it when they're not even eating. Which is unacceptable. So a few days ago, I started a power struggle to assert my right to be wherever I want in this house: every time they made me get down, I jumped right back up. They'd move me off the table, and I'd hop back on. Off, on, off, on...

Right now, Alice is napping, and I'm with the female two-leg who is scratching my head. On the table, of course.

Lineage

It's impossible! Absolutely impossible! Alice is standing up! I mean standing, like a two-leg. Granted, she's a little wobbly and balance isn't her strong suit, but she's on her feet! She fell down twice and she had a full-on *dontcry* crisis but with Mom and Dad's help, she got back up in no time.

This is throwing me off. I don't know what Alice is anymore. I always had doubts, but I'd settled on the idea she was some sort of Sphynx—albeit a weird one. As far as I know, though (admittedly I've never seen another Sphynx in my life, and I'm not sure why I even know they exist—but I'm a cat, so that should be enough of an explanation), Sphynxes do *not* walk on their hind legs. Only two-legs do that. And in fact, the more I watch Alice, the more she resembles the two-legs in a striking way. Even hair has started to sprout on her head— hair she definitely didn't have before—and that's not something you'd expect from a Sphynx.

I tried asking Felix what he thought, but the instant he saw Alice standing, he ran away in terror (which I sort of get), so he's no help in solving the mystery.

By logic, the situation is becoming clear. The hypothesis forming in my mind seems to be the only possible one: Alice is turning into a two-leg, which can only mean that two-legs must descend from Sphynxes.

Why?

Why am I here? Why am I stuck motionless in Alice's arms as she carries me around the house, laughing like I'm a sack of potatoes? Why am I no longer on the couch, where I was sleeping so peacefully?

And why, instead of stepping in—snatching me from these tiny but relentless arms—do Mom and Dad stand there laughing, looking all proud of the scene? Can someone explain what I've done to deserve this? Have I ever treated Alice badly? Did I bully Alice? Mock her? Of course not! So, can we please end this torture, restore some dignity to an adult cat, acknowledge the critical role I play in this household, and put a stop to this embarrassing farce?

It's not as though that coward, Felix—who spends his days under the bed—will step up and do something, at a minimum out of feline solidarity. Oh, no. He doesn't know the first thing about courage. As if he'd ever dreamed of intervening to save his brother or thinking of creating a diversion to distract this tiny extrem-ist, potentially a cat-exterminator in the making, and set me free. No—he just stays hidden while I watch my dignity slip away beneath my soft little paws.

Don't Even Think About It

Don't laugh. When I puff up my tail and arch my back, you're supposed to be scared. And if I hiss at you like I'm doing now, I want to see nothing but terror in your eyes. You have no idea what I might do in this state (to be fair, neither do I, but that's beside the point).

How dare you raise your voice at Alice? You made her have a *dontcry*, and that's not okay.

All I asked was for you to keep her from unintentionally hurting me, not to scold her for playing with me. That's something that should never happen again—got it, Mom? Figure out another way, make some plan, but Alice is off-limits. Otherwise, I'll throw up on the couch.

Doors

I've come to accept that two-legs are weird. They're not mean, far from it, but they have this compulsive need to surround themselves with useless, even harmful objects. Among their many oddities, doors are some of the hardest to grasp—especially how they relate to doors. I just don't get it. They've got these wonderful, spacious, bright areas, and what do they do? They install a door to block them off. But because blocking them off makes things dark and cramped, they leave them open.

I can't fathom the logic: why install something to close off an area if you don't actually want it closed in the first place? And not just one door, but many, wherever there's an opening. I guess it's none of my business—except it seriously limits my own freedom. When they go to the bathroom, for example, they tend to close the door (one of the very rare occasions), but that means I can't see what they're doing. And since that's when they're at their funniest, I want to watch. Luckily, one little meow is all it takes for them to open up. They're at least well-trained in that sense.

The other issue is with doors leading to the balcony. Here, it's clear they have an unhealthy obsession. I like being halfway in and halfway out—it makes me feel safe, and I like it. I don't have to explain myself to anyone. They can't wrap their heads around it. "Either in or out!" They can't conceive of a middle ground.

Sometimes I just stare at a door, and they don't get it. They ask what I'm looking at. Really, dear two-legs? I'm trying to figure out what's so special about these objects—why install so many objects designed to close off spaces that you actually want to keep open? Either we're dealing with some bizarre cult, or you've got serious issues.

Protection

Alice is really so tiny, for being a two-leg. She's like a two-leg cub, right after the Sphynx stage. When she walks, she wobbles; balance isn't her strong suit, and I'm always afraid she'll fall, which does happen sometimes.

When she laughs, she's the cutest thing, and I like going near her because her laughter sounds so delightful, even if she tends to grab me a bit too tightly.

She smells good, different from the adult two-legs—a much nicer scent, almost like perfume.

What I don't get is why they make her sleep alone in a little bed, with no one around in case of danger. What if there were night monsters? What if some dangerous creature breaks in under cover of darkness? The two-legs don't even consider this, but I'm definitely uneasy. So, starting tonight, I've decided to sleep in Alice's bed at her feet.

Don't worry, Alice. Whatever happens, I'll protect you.

Up Here

Why are you shouting? I'm right here. Not down there—up here, way up top. Does it seriously never occur to either of you to look up? I'm starting to take this personally, like you don't believe in my athletic abilities.—even though I'm pretty sure I've shown off my agility more than once. If you've already searched under every piece of furniture and every blanket, in every nook and cranny, maybe the next logical step is to lift your gaze.

It's not like you start to panic if I don't meow. I can't always be bothered to meow—sometimes you need to put in a bit of effort yourselves.

But no. I just can't understand you: how could I have fallen from the ledge of a closed window? How could I have escaped through a locked door? If you ask me, you're making fools of yourselves by shouting "Kitty-kitty" in front of everyone out on the street.

I think it's time to end this charade. I'll meow now, but let's be clear: I'm only doing this because I have no idea how to climb down from the top of this cabinet.

Ungrateful

What did I ever do to you?

Haven't I always treated you respectfully? I don't ask for much, and I'd say I make a pretty decent leader. I politely yet firmly let you know if something is off—be it a dirty litter box or an empty bowl—though frankly, you ought to check those things without my supervision.

In the evenings, I honor you with my presence on your laps and reward you with my purring. I try to avoid coughing up hairballs on the rug (unless it happens to be right under me, in which case it's not my fault), and I mostly use the scratching post for my claws. Mostly.

All in all, I think I'm the kind of cat many would love to have, so some of your behavior baffles me—it borders on cruelty.

After everything I do for you, can you tell me why you stopped brushing me when I clearly still wanted more?

Ungrateful!

The Dragon

Stop insisting. I won't indulge your reckless, childish whims. And believe me, I'm not coming out from under here. It's not that I don't trust you or Dad, but you both lack common sense.

Dragging that dragon around the house while it roars endlessly is a dangerous game. If it served some purpose, maybe I could understand, but what's the point of parading a dragon around with its snout pressed to the floor, breathing so loudly?

Sure, as long as you've got it under control, it might behave. But have you considered what would happen if it slipped out of your hands? Have you thought about the damage a rampaging dragon could do here? You two are big, but Felix and I are small—it could eat us! You're being selfish, caring only about your own entertainment. Have you noticed how ravenous it is? It even devours the tiniest crumbs on the floor, that's how insatiable it is!

So no, don't try telling me it's harmless. I'd rather be safe than risk my life because of your ridiculous recklessness.

Dual use

Why do two-legs clutter their home with useless objects? Why don't they share with us felines the admirable talent of recognizing more than one use for things?

We've already established they don't share our views on boxes: they throw them away, which is madness, because cardboard boxes make wonderfully cozy beds, as I can personally attest. Yet they discard them, trading them for cloth-based "beds" that are far less sturdy or protective. But I've accepted that. Yet have you seen how they react if you don't use the couch for lying down? The moment I try to sharpen my claws on it, they start yelling and chasing me off, as if they've lost their minds! Instead of calmly thanking me for finding a second use for their couch, they freak out…

And the table? They set it for meals, and if I hop on it to lounge for a bit—mind you not knocking anything over—they kick me off. If guests are there, they even apologize to them—Are they kidding? There's free space—why not use it? I honestly don't get it.

As for the rug, that's truly absurd. They lay it down to walk on when the floor's already there for walking. The rug is completely pointless if it can't serve a second purpose, and the moment I try to give it one—again, by sharpening my claws, which, let's face it, isn't like I have much else to do—they get mad.

And that's just the tip of the iceberg. I could go on and on. When they take off their clothes something they need to do because they have no fur, especially Mom and Alice (Dad has a bit more, but still not enough to keep warm), the most logical thing would be to let me nap on those clothes. But no! They claim I'd leave hair on them! But if they wear clothes to replace the fur they don't have, shouldn't they be grateful if I give them a bit more?

Even the fruit bowl, left empty—and I stress, empty—in the middle of the table, apparently can't be used as a cat bed. Obviously, if you remove the fruit from a fruit bowl, it's pointless. But they'd rather keep it empty than have me curled up inside. Same goes for the washing machine drum. I get not going in there when it's in use, but if it's just open, why can't I nap inside?

The closet deserves its own chapter. They don't want me in there, if I manage to slip in, they get mad and toss me out, yet three times they've locked me inside by mistake. Then, after a while (and after some very insistent meowing from me), they finally opened it, they showered me with kisses. They're strange—very strange.

All this runs through my head as they drag me away yet again just because I crawled into a shopping bag they left on the floor.

I'm speechless. Truly, I have no words.

Relief

They took Alice away. This morning, they got her all dressed up and left with her. It's happened before, but when they came back for lunch, she wasn't with them—and that's new.

I can't relax if I don't know where she is; it bothers me not to be able to protect her like I do at home and now I'm wondering if she'll return. I vaguely recall being separated from my birth family when I was little, and I don't want that happening to Alice. Mom and Dad two-leg seem calm, and all her stuff is still here, so I'm cautiously optimistic. But I'm not truly at ease. I've spent the day grooming myself to calm my nerves, while Felix seems to be enjoying the eerie silence in the house. It's late afternoon now, and normally, by this time, there's no peace whatsoever.

Wait, I think I hear something in the distance... Yes, I'm sure of it, that's definitely Alice's voice. No one else on earth reaches those ear-splitting pitches. What a relief!

I'm heading to the door to meet her. I bet she'll be thrilled to see me, probably pick me up and squeeze me a bit too much, but I'll get the comforting cuddles I need right now.

The Good Stuff

What a wonder… it's been a while since they managed to get their hands on this, but today's batch is really special. It's giving me this warm, blissful sensation in my brain—a real pleasant buzz. And it's fresh, just the way I like it.

No complaints here. When the catnip is that good, it's a total trip!

On the Run

They must not find me. I don't even know where Felix ended up. I saw him trying to hide somewhere safe, too, but in the chaos, we got separated. Our escape wasn't coordinated; we didn't even exchange a glance before fleeing the inhuman shrieks of these savages.

At first, we didn't realize how dire the situation was, so we let ourselves get caught briefly. Then we found ourselves surrounded by... I can't tell how many, but maybe ten of them: mini-two-legs, about Alice's height, who arrived with wrapped packages they used as bait to lure us into the open, only to turn on us.

When I finally wriggled free, not without a struggle, they chased me, blocked my escape routes, and tried to corner me. I heard Mom telling them to leave us alone, though I really wish she'd used a firmer, more commanding tone—this obviously didn't accomplish much. Maybe she knew from the start it was a lost cause.

I found a small space behind an armchair in the study, where I should be safe... They've found Felix! Hang in there, Felix, this torture will end eventually. They're holding him like a tube of toothpaste, passing him around. I can't watch—poor Felix. I just hope this ends soon, that their screams die down, and we can go back to normal. Whatever happens, Felix, know that in my own way, I cared about you.

Emptiness

This is not going well at all. We could stare at each other for hours, but it wouldn't change a thing: it's empty. Don't try to convince me otherwise. I have eyes, and I'm smart enough to see the obvious truth: it's empty.

You can stop pointing at the bottom of the bowl. I'm not about to stop meowing or eating in these pitiful conditions. That kibble is left over from yesterday—clearly just a cheap attempt to fool me. The bowl remains empty. It's "full" only when there's enough kibble to give me a sense of abundance. Right now, all I sense is pathetic emptiness. Enough talk—do your job and fill that bowl!

Sadness

Something must have happened to my two-legs—I've never seen them like this. They're so quiet. Sometimes Dad looks sadder than anyone else when he's having a *dontcry*. Maybe it's because one of the older female two-legs, who seemed really close to him, hasn't come around in a while. Tonight, they sat on the couch, but they haven't turned on that magic picture box they usually watch. They lit a candle and talked to God—this time politely, without blaming him. God must be someone very important to them. I'm glad he's on my side and takes the blame for me.

While they were talking to God, Dad was consumed by a powerful *dontcry*, and then everyone was sucked into the *dontcry*. I was on the floor watching them, unsure what to do. Then I remembered they often keep little bits of paper on the nightstand to wipe their tears. So I went to the bedroom, grabbed that little packet of tissues in my mouth, and brought it to them.

When they saw me, they praised me a lot and their *dontcry* became even more intense than before. Then they picked me up and placed me between them on the couch, showering me with cuddles. After that, they went back to talking with God. I don't really know what to say to God since I've never met him and don't understand who he is, but I like him, so I stayed right there with them.

The Gift

I've been staring out of this window for years now. Rain or shine, hot or cold, the two-legs are always on the move—either on foot or in those awful, noisy boxes on wheels. At first, I couldn't figure out why they'd rush around, but as I got older, it became clear: kibble doesn't grow on trees, so someone has to hunt it down.

I've concluded they do all this for us cats. Every person I see out there must have a cat at home waiting to be fed every day, and that's why they're always in such a hurry. Let's face it: kibble is tiny and probably hides really well. Once they catch it, they trap it in plastic bags so it can't escape anymore, and by the time it reaches us, it's already lifeless.

I've never seen live kibble. I often wonder what it looks like—well, not often, maybe two or three times in my whole life, since the topic doesn't fascinate me. I only care that it's in my bowl when I'm hungry. I can't quite imagine how it moves—maybe it bounces, maybe it crawls. It might roll, but that seems unlikely. Could it swim? Or fly? It might swim, but I doubt it can fly. I've seen everything in my life—pigeons, sparrows, crows, bats, flies, bees, mosquitoes—so if a kibble could fly, I'd have noticed.

Whatever it looks like or whatever it does, I have a lot of respect for the two-legs who hunt it down. Mom and Dad have never let me or Felix or even Mama Mimi (before she left and never came back) go without. That's why I decided it was only right to show them my gratitudde. And that's why, just a while ago, I brought them a lizard I caught on the balcony (which stays open on warm nights). I made sure not to kill it so it would be extra fresh. It was still bleeding a bit when I left it on their pillow.

I admit I wasn't expecting such an such an overwhelming display of joy: the moment they saw it, both two-legs let out a shout of excitement and practically leapt out of bed, fighting each other for the lizard and racing out of the room with it—probably to eat it in private.

They told me I shouldn't have done that, but Mom, Dad, it wasn't a duty! It was a pleasure, straight from my heart. And given your enthusiasm, I promise I'll bring you more from time to time.

My World

Do you ever wonder, Felix, what's out there—beyond what we see through the window? No? Never ever? I do, sometimes, and it scares me. Years ago, when I fell off the balcony, I remember everything was so different from here, noisy, filled with unfamiliar smells I'd never encountered.

You know what the worst part was? I was alone. It was a terrible feeling, almost worse than being afraid, because sure, I get scared sometimes, but I've never truly been alone my whole life. And being alone, in the dark, somewhere you don't know—that's the most unpleasant feeling I've ever had. For me, snuggling in Mom or Dad's lap at night is reassuring, and when I'm with them, I can sleep soundly, knowing nobody will harm me. With Alice, I try to keep one eye open to protect her, but she's so big now, I think she might actually be the one protecting me. And that's okay with me. I like my world just the way it is, I'm happy here with my two-legs and even with you, Felix…

Felix… hey… you dozed off again? How can you sleep all the time? I swear…

Oh well, never mind. Scoot over a bit so I can cuddle up. There's nothing else we can do right now but nap. And honestly, I'm happy with that.

Felix

Felix is getting older. I'm not sure how old he is—maybe a bit older than me and much younger than Mama Mimi was. We never really clicked; our personalities are too different. Sometimes we played together, and occasionally we napped side by side, all curled up. But for the most part, we keep different habits.

Felix sleeps more than I do, which isn't a minor feat, because I love sleeping and will indulge that passion anytime. But he outdoes me by far. I have to admit, though, that ever since Mama Mimi left, he's become a bit sad.

They were very close, and for days after she disappeared, he was down and glum.

Also, Felix barely ever jumps—I rarely see him higher than the bed. He's happy enough to eat, but unlike me, he never asks for food. If the bowl is empty, he waits for someone to notice and fill it on their own. Sometimes I suspect he relies on me to complain and make sure nobody forgets to fill the bowl, because I definitely won't stand for that.

Look, I adore the two-legs, but honestly, they don't have that many responsibilities—just two or three main tasks: hunt kibble, fill our kibble dish, fill the water bowl, clean the litter box, and pet us when we want. Doesn't sound like such a busy life that they can't feed two cats.

But that's just Felix—he's fine with anything, never complains—except when Alice used to pick him up and squeeze him like a rag. Now that she's grown, even that doesn't bother him. Loud noises, though, especially storms, freak him out.

During storms—or especially that evening a few days after they drag in the fake tree, when suddenly every two-leg in the world decides to make noise at once—Felix hides. You can tell he's miserable: he trembles all over, and there's no coaxing him out. Usually, he crawls under the bedcovers, and we can spot him easily because his silhouette is so obvious. Then again, Felix's never been great at finding hiding places—or at anything, really. Still, he's a good guy, and even though we've never been super close, we do share a bond, and I care about him—whatever that means. Sometimes when I'm not feeling great, Felix picks up on it and he comes right over to nap beside me.

Abandonment

I don't know what's happening to me. I feel sick and can hardly breathe.

I've never felt like this before, and I'm at a loss. Mom and Dad are looking for me, and even Alice is calling me. I managed to slip into a hidden nook behind some clothes. I'm scared, and I don't want them to see me like this—who knows what they would think? At the same time, I'm hoping they find me because I just want them to hold me and cuddle me the way they always do, so this might all vanish like magic, and I can breathe normally again. I want everything to go back to normal, like waking up from a bad dream.

I can sense how worried they are; they're tearing the house apart trying to find me. Maybe I should meow so they can find me, but I just don't have the energy. And I'm terrified of what might happen if this nightmare turns out to be real.

Oh, they're in the room now, right nearby, rummaging around… yes, here they are. They've found me.

Mom picked me up, and I saw fear in her eyes. Dad's eyes too. And Alice had a good *dontcry* while she petted my head.

They're putting me in the cage. By now I know exactly where we're headed. Over the years, I've learned that when I go in the cage, we usually end up at that place with the bearded man in the white coat and glasses who always tries to stick needles in me.

And this time must be something special, because I've done my business in the carrier again (old habits die hard), and Dad hasn't yelled at his God. In fact, he told me it's fine and that I should stay calm. But I can't calm down: I've always liked God because he takes the blame instead of me. If Dad isn't blaming him this time, it might mean that God's gone and no longer here with me. I've never seen him, but the thought of God abandoning me is terrifying.

Exhaustion

"Cancer." I don't know exactly what that means, but judging by Mom, Dad, and Alice's reaction, it can't be good. I'm guessing it's the cause of my pain and my trouble breathing because they did something called "chemo"—at least that's what I think they said—to see if it would go away.

We're on our way home now. I do feel slightly better, but I'm not sure if it's the chemo or just that they're all showering me with extra cuddles. They're feeding me special kibble—the fancy variety they catch only occasionally—which tastes better than the others. But honestly, I want cuddles more than food right now. I'd love to sleep once we're back. I haven't gotten much sleep these past few days.

At least I'm breathing a bit easier, so maybe this annoying thing is improving. Now I'm going to jump on the couch and lie down next to Alice, and rest. Mom and Dad will be near me, and even Felix is hovering, not wanting to leave. I'm so tired. I just want to sleep and wake up feeling better, like none of this ever happened.

Go Ahead and Cry

The night didn't go well. I woke up struggling for air, my whole body hurting. I jumped off the bed and hid again, partly because I'm scared, partly because I hate them seeing me like this. My mouth is hanging open to breathe, which I never do, but I feel like I'm suffocating if I don't.

Either way, they found me right away. Now they know all my hiding spots, and I just can't muster the creativity to find new ones. It's still dark out, all three of them are having a *dontcry*, but none of them is pointing it out to the others, as if in this moment a *dontcry* all together was normal. They're staying close, petting me, but this time I'm not reassured. It's not enough to stop my fear.

Eventually, I see sunlight breaking through the darkness. From the couch, I can glimpse the window where I've spent so many hours staring outside.

I get this odd feeling—I want to look out at least one more time, watch the sun rise as I love to do, but I can't move. A strange certainty overcomes me: I'll never see the world from that window again.

Dad is on the phone with someone, and I know he's talking about me from the way he looks at me. Now he's stopped talking, turned to Mom, and they both walked over to Alice, who's holding me tight but not hurting me.

They must have told her something bad— Alice is consumed by a huge *dontcry*, I guess that's what they call "crying," because Mom and Dad told her "Go ahead and cry." It's the first time I've heard them use that word, and it sounds so much sadder than the *dontcry*.

And now what are you doing? Oh no, not the cage again—Mom, Dad, no, please—let's not go back there! I know you think you're doing this for my sake, but they did all sorts of things to me yesterday, and it didn't help at all... Can't I just stay here at home? I don't feel safe over there, and I don't want them doing weird stuff to me anymore.

No need to latch the cage, I'll settle at the back on my own. I won't run. I don't have the strength.

Stay Close

This place is terrible. The table is so cold and gray—or maybe it just feels that way because, for the first time, I hear the three of you crying. Really crying. Or maybe it's because I can barely breathe. I'm looking for a window so I can see the sun I love so much, but there is none here, no sunlight. What's happening, Mom? Dad? Alice?

Here comes the man in the white coat. I have no idea what he just told you, but this time the needle he's holding looks really strange. Alice, how many kisses are you giving me? And your tears feel so warm, your gentle strokes feel sweeter than ever. Mom and Dad's caresses are soothing, too. It's like I've never needed them more than right now.

I've never liked needles, and I like this one even less. What is he injecting me with? What's this feeling? Everything's going fuzzy, my vision's going dark. I can barely make out Mom, Dad, and Alice. Actually, I can't see them at all now.

I'm scared, so scared. Please stay close. Please don't stop petting me. Keep going, keep going, and now—oh, the pain is fading, but I can't see anymore. Don't leave me, I can't move, I can't hear anything, it's all empty. Stay with me, pet me, don't go away.

Don't leave me alone.

Epilogue

What's this place? How did I get here? I only remember a sort of rainbow bridge, but maybe I dreamed it. I've seen this place before, but I can't remember when. And where did all these thousands upon thousands of cats come from? I'm so confused...

But wait, that's you...Mama Mimi!

Mama!!!

I knew we'd meet again someday—I just knew it. This is wonderful!

But where are we, Mama? Why do I feel like I've been here before? Oh, right! This is that place I used to glimpse when I sat on that special tile and stared into emptiness, not knowing what I was seeing…

And that one over there, winking at me with a smile—I've never seen him, but I know exactly who he is! He's the one who always took the blame in my place, Dad's "God"!

What's this place called, Mama? "The Waiting Room"? That's a funny name… and what are we waiting for? Wait, seriously??? Are Mom, Dad, and Alice going to come for us? That's amazing. When?

…

But that's ages from now! It's so much longer than I even lived. By the time they get here, they'll have forgotten us. That's way too long.

Oh, you're saying not once has a two-leg ever forgotten their cat?

Never ever ever?

Really really really?

And Felix will arrive a lot sooner, you say? Well, that makes me feel better. At least all three of us can wait together.

But I'm still a little sad. How about I go sit by that windowsill over there while we wait? I know there's a lot of time left, but maybe it works both ways—if I find just the right tile and stare into the distance, I might see them again.

And who knows, maybe in the meantime, the sun will rise…

Acknowledgements

A special thanks to Luisa, Martina, Michel, Placidia, Sabrina, Serena and Silvia, who previewed parts of this book—without knowing who wrote theM—and who encouraged me to keep going with my writing.

Table of Contents